30 Days of Learning to Love YOU

2nd Edition + 60 Days of Infinite Blessings - Guided Journals

By
Rebecca J Lee

This book is dedicated to my children, Ben, Sarah, and Veronica. Without you I would not be here. You were Moonbeams in my dark night and now you are my Sun Rays warming me in my Happy Days.

"There are two kinds of suffering: The suffering that leads to more suffering and the suffering that leads to the end of suffering. If you are not willing to face the second kind of suffering, you will surely continue to experience the first."

\-   Ajahn Chah, A Still Forest Pool

(This quote is found at the beginning of my favorite book Dancing with Life by Phillip Moffit)

30 Days of Learning to Love YOU

A Guided Journal Experience
Rewritten 2018

About This Journal

I wrote this journal because I find the greatest joy in encouraging others. I don't have a degree or any special training but, I do have life experience.

My life has been full of hardship and joy. However, until a few years ago, I mainly saw the hardship and rarely experienced joy.

In August of 2012 I divorced the father of my 3 beautiful children. I was already broken but, the trauma of divorce forced me to sink or swim. I decided to swim.

At first, I only managed to dog paddle and often had fits of flailing about, sure I was doomed to drown. However, counseling and a slew of self-help books led me to the successful swimming techniques I use today.

I wrote this to inspire you to find 'swimming techniques' of your own. I doubt anyone can benefit from everything I write here because we're all unique. I caution you to follow my example with care. Please work with a therapist if you are experiencing trauma or are fresh from a storm.

I have included lined pages for writing thoughts and insights. I hope this will help you discover the practices to help you live your best life.

Without further ado, here's a 30-day peek at what my 'swimming' looks like these days.

DAY 1

Going through my divorce was good for me because it helped me see my many toxic beliefs. The most toxic was the idea that it was no big deal to berate and bully myself. I didn't even realize how awful I was being to myself until I heard someone say that we are often our own worst enemy.

I disagreed! I thought I loved myself. Sure, I might feel the need to lose a few pounds or stop drinking so much coffee but that's just wanting to push myself to be a better person. Right?

Then, the challenge came, "If you wouldn't say it to your best friend, don't say it to yourself."

Fine! Challenge accepted!

Wow! What an eye opener! I didn't last 5 minutes before spilling something and calling myself stupid. Once I realized how mean I was to myself, my negative self-talk, ironically, spiraled out of control. I couldn't stop the negative thoughts no matter how hard I tried. I ended up giving up on the whole idea of not saying to myself what I wouldn't say to others. I decided these negative thoughts weren't hurting anyone if I wasn't saying them to someone else; especially since they were about me.

Years later I discovered a practice that would free me from this toxic belief. I figured out that I was trying to stop judging myself by judging my thoughts. No wonder it didn't work. I learned to observe my thoughts and then instead of berating myself for negative thoughts, I just challenged the thoughts without labeling them as bad. I would ask, "Is this true? Am I stupid for spilling milk?". This helped me focus on the answer rather than judging myself for the initial negative thought. This technique worked best when I stuck to facts. "I'm not stupid. I spilled the milk because I'm moving too fast. I should slow down, so I don't spill anything else."

Speaking of slowing down, it works magic on stopping negative self-talk. When I rush around, I stress myself out. When I slow down, I make fewer mistakes. No mistakes mean no reason for negative thoughts to creep in. It also means less time spent on cleaning up 'spilled milk'.

Here's my challenge for today:

1. I will give myself extra time to get ready for my day. I'll take some time to really enjoy little blessings, like coffee and walks with my toy poodle, Xena. I'll do the most important things first and give myself permission to not finish everything on my to do list because I know the world will not end if I don't get it all done.
2. I'll remind myself that when I use mindfulness as I work, tasks take less time because I make fewer mistakes when I do things thoughtfully.
3. Finally, I'll compliment myself on a job well done even if I think I failed today's challenge. I know I can't fail because my attempt is enough to prove I want a better life. This is Loving Me!

Tonight, I will answer the following questions:
1. How did it feel to slow down?
2. What tasks can I do each day, mindfully, to remind myself to slow down? (Washing my hands counts)
3. What can I say to myself to acknowledge my efforts and progress?

I'm finally okay with seeing the good in myself. I can see that being boastful is seeing myself as better than others, while healthy pride in myself holds no comparison to others. It is an essential step toward becoming my own best friend.

DAY 2

Today I want to look at how I determine my worth. I've come to see that where I don't judge the worth of others based on their abilities, looks, or intelligence, I do judge myself based on my abilities, looks, and intelligence.

I'm able to let go of seeing my worth this way when I acknowledge that my worth isn't based on my weight, degree, material possessions, or anything else. My worth is dependent on my actions and beliefs. Life is better for all when I can stop focusing on the physical and instead look to my spirit for my worth.

However, I must be careful to only look at today and to let go of regret and self-loathing for mistakes made in my past. Judging myself based on my past only makes my current actions and beliefs more negative. Instead, I do my best to look ahead and decide what I can do today to be a better me.

Today, I will try to focus on loving all those around me unconditionally. This includes loving myself flaws and all!

Journal Prompt for today:
1. How do I feel when thinking negative thoughts about myself?
2. How can I respond to those thoughts in a way that will help me embrace who I am now?

DAY 3

Yesterday, I talked about how I have learned to embrace my flaws. As hard as it was for me to learn how to embrace my flaws, it was even harder for me to acknowledge my good traits without feeling like I was being prideful. However, I finally came to understand that being prideful comes from thinking I'm better than others whereas being thankful for my uniqueness and being amazed at the uniqueness of others is a vital part of loving myself!

So, in the interest of learning to love myself, I will identify 3 of my favorite attributes.

I'm going to refrain from focusing on my physical traits. It would be a good exercise to list my 3 favorite physical characteristics, however, today, I want to dig deeper!

Here's a list I put together to help with this exercise:

1. Who do I love and what do I love about them? Is it their compassion, hardworking attitude, loyalty, or resilience? Do I have some of these same characteristics?
2. What do I love to do? Do I like to hike, cook, color, draw, sing, write, play video games, watch movies, or sit quietly with my pets or out in nature? Do I love to shop? I can use these things to help me see what my talents are. For instance, if I love to shop I bet I can spot a good deal a mile away or put together an outfit that would make celebrities swoon! If I love reading, movies, or video games, it's probable that I'm a creative soul and a dreamer who can change the world by imagining a better future!

3. What sensations do I enjoy the most? Do I love my gift of sight and find myself gazing at the sky or art, etc.? Do I adore music or the sound of the ocean? Do I love the way silk feels on my skin? How about the scents or tastes I enjoy? What talents are associated with these? The appreciation of any of these is a positive and worthwhile attribute!

Journal Prompt for today:
What are the things I like most about me?

*I give myself bonus points for being able to take a compliment. If someone says something nice about me it's because they see that quality in me. If I deny their compliment I invalidate their opinion. Now, I can just smile and say, "Thank you!"

DAY 4

Have you ever worked for someone or had a teacher or friend who just expected too much? Maybe, they didn't understand what they were asking of you or maybe they were just too selfish to care.

When this happens to me I feel like all my efforts aren't good enough. This person doesn't appreciate how much I'm already doing.

But what if the person asking is me? Every day, I demand so much from myself. It's okay to push my limits so I can stretch and grow. But, I also need to appreciate how far I've already come. If I acknowledge my progress, I'll be motivated to keep pushing forward.

Today, as I go about getting things done I'm going to stop and be grateful for each accomplishment, no matter how small. I'll take a moment to smile and acknowledge that I'm doing my best and moving forward.

By the way, I count eating, drinking, and taking care of my hygiene. I must do these things to keep going and taking care of myself is vital!

Journal Prompt for today:
Write down a few things you've done this week that really needed doing. Give yourself credit for all that you do every day.

DAY 5

Today I will look at how firmly I hold onto my expectations and how doing this can give my inner critic way too much material to work with.

When I hold onto expectations of how life should be, I often miss the blessings sitting right in front of me. When I'm feeling disappointed I try to stop and look at what my expectations were. I try to see if they were unreasonable or if there was something I didn't think of when forming my expectations.

For instance, when it's a person who disappoints me, I likely misunderstood their abilities, beliefs, or resources. Or maybe I misunderstood the role they play in my life. Perhaps they weren't meant to meet the need I was expecting them to meet; or at least, not in the way or timing I was expecting.

The truth is I never need to be disappointed again! I can enjoy my life more fully when I realize life is as it is and, then choose to love my life no matter what! Doing this sets me up to find happiness whether my expectations are met or not. I'm only miserable when I can't let go of expectations. I found so much freedom when I learned to let my expectations go! Or to say it another way, I learned to let the specifics of my expectations go. I expect to be happy and when happiness comes in a different form than I expect, I don't stay stuck on my idea of how the happiness should've come. Because if I do I'll miss out on joyful moments right in front of me.

Journal Prompt for today:
What is one disappointment I've experienced? How can I change my perspective to see the blessing that was there all along?

DAY 6

This week I've shared how I find ways to quiet the inner critic and stop negative self-talk. Today, I want to share a unique perspective that helps me connect with my negative side. It may sound strange but, that negativity comes from some broken place inside me. If I just ignore it that part of me will stay broken.

So, I visualize my inner critic as a child who is just feeling insecure and acting out. I visualize sitting with that child, wrapping my arms around her, and having compassion for her. I honor the emotions that she's bringing to my attention and I tell her that I hear what she's trying to say. Then, I let her know she's safe and loved.

This may sound weird, but it works. Sometimes I think growing up we get the message that our feelings aren't okay. When we got angry, or sad, or afraid, maybe someone who didn't know what to say just told us to stop feeling like that and just be happy. The problem with this is that children don't know how to change their feelings any more than we do. They end up feeling like they're bad because of the emotion they're experiencing. It's important to tell that inner child that they're not bad no matter what emotion they're having. Even though I'm talking to myself, it's important for me to tell myself that I'll always love me.

Is this a strange concept? It was for me, at first. But then I realized that I'm the only person I'm with ALL the time. I need to have my back because no one else can be there for me the way I can. I want to be my own best friend because I've learned that doing this makes me a better person and I have so much more to give those around me than I've ever had before.

Journal Prompt for today:
How did it feel to honor my inner critic?

DAY 7

Today, I'm going to take some time to think over this past week.

Day 1 - I focused on slowing down.
Day 2 - I focused on learning to embrace my flaws.
Day 3 - I focused on appreciating my talents.
Day 4 - I focused on being reasonable with what I expect of myself.
Day 5 - I focused on letting go of expectations.
Day 6 - I focused on having compassion for my inner critic.

Journal Prompt for today:
I will write a few sentences on how this week went. What were my biggest wins?

DAY 8

This week I want to talk about how I embrace my mistakes. My mistakes hold a treasure trove of blessings I can use to make my life beautiful. Mistakes are not bad. Progress can't happen without them.

What is a mistake, anyway? A mistake is any action that results in an unwanted result or a result other than what is considered correct.

For instance, have you ever bought a car that turned out to be a lemon and thought, 'Well, that was a mistake!'. This would be a mistake in judgement. You wouldn't have bought the car knowing it was going to cause you mechanical headaches. On the other hand, you may be trying to learn a new skill. With any new skill, there are bound to be hundreds, or thousands of mistakes made along the way to perfecting the skill.

I think of the art of living as a skill. As I perfect this art, I'll undoubtedly, make many mistakes. I'll misjudge others and they will misjudge me. This is just life and we're all doing our best to learn how to live it.

However, there've been times when I've become so discouraged with my progress that I wanted to give up completely because I wanted better results, faster. I got tired of having to correct mistakes. But then I realized my problem. I was comparing my progress with the progress of others. This is silly because my life and my skill set is so different from everyone else's.

For example, when I was young I tried to learn how to play the violin. I was so discouraged with my progress that in class one day I broke into tears. I was comparing my progress with students who had more experience and with my incredibly talented teacher. My sweet teacher pointed out that it takes us all a long time to master new skills and that it took her many years to get the hang of playing her own violin.

This has stuck with me. Whenever, I'm trying to learn something new, I remember her words and I have patience with myself. I don't compare my house keeping skills, budgeting, parenting skills, or anything else with anyone else's skills. I can learn from others, but I shouldn't judge myself from where they are in their journey. I need to look at where I am and be proud of how far I have come!

Journal Prompt for today:
I will write a few sentences about something in life I'm struggling with and how I can be a bit more patient with myself.

Remember, You Are Amazing! Just keep going!

DAY 9

Yesterday I talked about how comparing myself to others can lead to me feeling like a failure. Comparison can also lead to me being judgmental.

When I can learn to let go of judgement it becomes far easier for me to embrace my mistakes and the mistakes of others.

One surprising thing I've discovered is that the way I feel about mistakes is strongly connected to the resentment I'm holding onto. Resentment seemed to be about what others are doing to me. But as I've allowed love to work on my heart I found that resentment wasn't at all about the misdeeds of others or their mistakes. My resentment of others is about how I'm unable to cope with my own inability to feel worthy.

Let me try and explain it a better way. I often felt that I supported others in my life way more than they supported me. I felt like if I do this for them then they should do the same for me. Right?

Well, it seems like an innocent enough assumption, but the problem is we're all too unique to be able to support each other in the same ways. Because I didn't take this into consideration I allowed resentment to poison my relationships. Finally, I realized that the only one responsible for my happiness is me. And what does this have to do with my feeling worthy?

I deserve to be happy. I am 'worthy' of happiness. If I don't believe this I can't do things to make myself happy without feeling guilty. I will keep doing for others without considering myself and this will ultimately make me resentful. This is because when I do things to make others happy without considering my own happiness I put the responsibility of my happiness on them. If they don't do as much for me as I do for them, I will resent them.

Here's the deal - When we can see mistakes or inadequacies as valuable tools, it becomes easier to look within and work on ourselves. The need to blame others for not being there for us begins to fade away.

Journal Prompt for today:
Think of 3 people who have let you down.
1. Who are they and what did they do or not do?
2. Why do you feel it was their responsibility to support you in this situation?
3. How can you see where this was a blessing in disguise? Perhaps this situation led to you discovering inner strength or gave you the motivation to do healing work inside yourself?

Be kind to yourself today. These are not easy subjects to work on. Try to expect less of yourself than what you do normally because working on yourself is HUGE and requires a lot of physical energy to get through!

DAY 10

Once I took responsibility for my own happiness I was able to look at my mistakes and short comings in a new way. I began to love myself regardless of what I was doing well or not so well. This freed me to see the treasure inside each of my mistakes.

Here's the deal: The first piece of treasure in every mistake is the knowledge that I'm one step closer to reaching my goal. Every journey has a certain number of steps and a certain number of trips and falls. It's inevitable. When I trip I can take solace knowing I'm one trip-up closer to perfection.

The second treasure is the wisdom hidden in that mistake. There have been so many times where I missed the wisdom in a mistake because I was too prideful to take responsibility. I let life bring me the same situation over and over and I responded the same way each time, so I never got anywhere. I felt like a hamster on a wheel. Finally, I stopped and let my mistake guide me toward making better choices. For example, I realized I was accepting dates from toxic people. I asked myself why and figured out that since I lived in a toxic relationship for so long that was what I was used to and what felt comfortable to me. Then, I took a good look at my self-worth and did my best to work on me before trying to share my love with someone else.

There are many treasures lying in your mistakes too. The last one I'll talk about is the treasure of our uniqueness. Making mistakes is a natural part of life and they color our world and become our story. Don't hide your story! Others can learn from it! And when you fall get back up! You can be the inspiration to help others do the same!

Journal Prompt for today:
Think about the last mistake you've made. Can you apply these ideas to find your own treasure?

DAY 11

Today I want to focus on how I view problems. I used to see problems as bad, miserable things that held me back from happiness and kept my head under water. But this view only served to make me miserable! So now, I choose to see my problems as opportunities to learn something new.

One reason problems are seen negatively is the fear of making a mistake. See if this is true for you. Take a problem you're facing today and see if you can remove the fear of making a mistake. Does doing this help make the problem seem easier to deal with?

Here's the deal:
I have found that I make far less mistakes and get further down my path when I let go of fear. So, when I look at my problems I do my best to take fear out of the equation.

Journal Prompt for today:
1. Factually, define the problem.
2. Factually, define the options.
3. Ask your heart how it feels about the situation.
4. What you can learn from this situation?
5. Plan and fearlessly go forward!

My idea of being brave is wanting to run but deciding to stay!

DAY 12

One major advantage to embracing my mistakes is that it allows me to fearlessly go forward!

When I know that mistakes make up so much of the spice of life, I can embrace them, knowing they make life fun, interesting, and the truly wondrous learning experience life is meant to be!

Give yourself permission to make these wondrous slip ups that can make your life more fun and fulfilled than you ever thought possible!

Journal Prompt for today:
List three things you would do if you knew you couldn't fail:
(Here are a few examples)
1. Learn to Tango
2. Start your dream business
3. Leave your responsibilities for a while and take that trip, already!

Now, list 3 reasons you aren't already working toward these dreams or if you're already working towards them, what is holding you back from doing even more to get where you truly want to go?

Here are some common reasons:
1. My family depends on me and I'm afraid of letting them down.
2. People will judge me.
3. I don't have the resources I need to get started.

Are any of these reasons being colored by your fear of failure?

What baby step can you take toward your dreams?

DAY 13

What are you dreaming of? Or are you dreaming at all? Have you been lulled into the mundane trance of bills and responsibilities?

We must pay bills and take care of our responsibilities but too often these things become our entire existence. If this happens we can become vulnerable to despair, resentment, depression, fear, and anxiety.

Let me help you breathe life back into the core reason you are paying those bills and tending those responsibilities! Let's get back to the business of living life, instead of just enduring it!

I found freedom many years ago when I let go of the 'I have to' syndrome. I finally realized, that truly, there is nothing I 'have' to do. I can sit on the floor and drool all day, and while that would be utterly boring and the nice men in white coats would surely come get me, this is my choice. So, take back your choice! You don't 'have to' do anything! Re-examine your 'whys'. Why do you choose to do the things you do? You may discover that there are many things you're doing that you hate doing and have no good reason for doing them!

Journal Prompt for today:
Take a minute and list out a few things you feel are your responsibility.

Next to each of these, write out why you feel so compelled to do them.

Re-evaluate each one and decide whether it can be shared with someone, given to someone else completely, or let go of, all together, for the sake of your happiness and sanity!

Finally, do some thinking about what your passions are. Are there baby steps you can take toward finding your way back to them?

DAY 14

How did this week feel for you? We covered quite a bit in one short week!

1. We talked about zapping resentment.
2. We examined the progress mistakes bring.
3. We looked at treasures found in our mistakes.
4. We looked at problems in a positive light, so we are not afraid of mistakes.
5. We listed three things we'd do if fear were not a factor.
6. Finally, yesterday, we dug even deeper, examining what holds us back from going after our dreams.

Tomorrow, we will begin a week of tearing away the expectations that no longer serve us; many of which, probably never served us. These are expectations we have of ourselves, as well as, the expectations others have of us.

Journal Prompt for today:

Take a few minutes to think back on this past week.

What really stood out for you?

Why?

Keep Going! You're Doing Great!

P.S. Take some time today to be mindful. Observe your senses as you wash dishes or listen to your child, friend, or loved one talk. Just spend, at least a few minutes, observing your world and soaking it all in. We are here to live so let's get living!

DAY 15

This week I'm focusing on expectations. I'll look at the expectations I have for myself and the expectations placed on me by others.

For today, spend a few minutes thinking about what you expect from yourself.

Do you make to do list that you expect to complete in an unreasonable amount of time? Are you forever thinking errands and chores will take way less time than they take? Do you expect projects to be done quickly and then find they take much longer?

If yes, do you blame yourself, your lack of resources and/or support or even other people for not being able to accomplish things faster? I used to do this ALL THE TIME! And, I still catch myself wishing I could fit more into my schedule than is humanly possible!

However, I'm becoming much better at letting go of expecting so much out of 24 hours. I have turned it around so that I celebrate every time I get something done, instead of berating myself for the things that still need doing.

As I learn to let go of unreasonable expectations, I have discovered I am no longer stressed out, moody, and anxious.

This week, I will show you how doing this can also lead to finding your passions and taking steps toward bringing them to life!

Journal Prompt for today:

1. List a few expectations you have for today that may be unreasonable.
2. List those things that are really stressing you out.
3. How are these things being affected by unreasonable expectations?

DAY 16

Things are the way they are. Wishful thinking will not change anything. It's a trap that will have you missing all the amazing things that are already in your life.

Don't get me wrong. Dreaming and thinking about a better tomorrow can be a wonderful tool. Used in moderation, it will add joy to your life and lead you to the 'better tomorrow' you are dreaming of. The problem comes when you stay in the state of dreaming all the time or too much of the time. Another pit fall is trying to figure out all the how's to your dream and deciding what must happen to make your dream come true. Again, doing this can be healthy, when used carefully.

Here's the deal:
Do not obsess over how things 'should' be. When you come across something that you feel is 'wrong' and there is nothing you can do about it right now, let it go. Focus, instead on the things that are 'right'.

Examples of this would be heavy traffic, health problems, other people's actions, wishing you had a better car or house, etc.

Note - There are things you can do for all the examples I listed. The point is not to ignore your problems. The point is to not obsess over them.

Journal Prompt for today:
1. Give an example of something you tend to obsess over that you can't change.
2. What blessing is hiding there? or What blessing can you focus on instead?
3. What practical steps can you take to help yourself let go of how things 'should be' so that you can enjoy how things are?

For example - practicing mindful driving, focusing on pleasant sensations, finding positive attributes in others, practicing gratitude for all you have.

Remember, be patient with yourself through this process! Do what you can and leave the rest for later!

DAY 17

I think the number one reason we hold onto our expectations, so much is because we really wish we knew what comes next. We want everyone to follow a set of social rules and do what is generally considered 'normal' and 'right'. If they do this, we feel safe because we're all following the same rules and we all know what to expect from each other.

If someone veers away from 'normal' we feel insecure because now we don't know what we can expect from them. It's scary. That's why we shy away from what is different or strange.

When we realize that all expectations are a security issue it becomes . easier to understand the unreasonable expectations others have for us and that we have for ourselves. We will even begin seeing where our own expectations of others are sometimes unreasonable.

Maybe you don't see it this way? But think about it. Why do we get so upset when things are not the way they 'should' be? For example, I get super anxious if my bank account is too low. When I pay my bills on time I know exactly what to expect. Things run smoothly. If I start making payments late my future begins to become uncertain. My security is shaken.

The next time you find yourself judging someone, ask yourself what you're so afraid of. For instance, if you judge others because of their weight, are you afraid of being judged for your appearance? If you judge someone for their possessions are you afraid of being judged as unsuccessful because of your house, car, clothes, etc.?

Usually we judge others because we are afraid of being judged ourselves.

This is because we need each other. We need connection. If others judge us, we are afraid of losing that connection. The ironic thing is, the more we fear losing this connection, the weaker our connection to others becomes!

Let go of the fear of being judged and you will experience the strongest connection to others (all others)! It's incredible!

Journal Prompt for today - answer the following:
1. What one thing am I the most afraid of being judged for?
2. Do I know of others who have this same 'flaw'?
3. How can having compassion for myself and others give me a stronger connection to those around me?

DAY 18

Today, focus on loosening your grip on, both, the expectations of others and the importance you place on what others expect of you.

Do this by having compassion for yourself and others.

Don't drop your dreams and goals. Rather, watch them unfold. Let the future play out without adding stress by placing judgment on how it is unfolding.

For example, if you were to take a vacation with loved ones, it would be easy to compare how things go with how you want them to go. So, if you took a tour of some caves and the guide was rude, you could make the experience better by having compassion, first, for yourself and your loved ones (who are likely annoyed at having to spend time and money to put up with this person). And then, have compassion for the tour guide, knowing they may be going through challenges in life that feel unbearable to them. Or perhaps they are allowing stress to make them cranky.

Next, you could act according to the compassion you have for everyone. Be kind and gentle to all involved so you don't add stress to the situation.

We tend to get defensive when we are treated rudely. This only adds to our stress and the stress of everyone around us. Instead, take rude behavior in stride. It's fine to speak up and not put up with the rude behavior. But do so with compassion.

Journal Prompt for today:
Think of a situation where someone was rude to you and you reacted rudely back. How did this affect the situation? Or, think of a situation where someone was rude, and you reacted with kindness. How did this affect the situation?

Day 19

Today can be your day of liberation.

What I'm about to share with you has changed my world. It has abolished my fears and breathed life back into my life journey. Do this one thing and I promise you will be free!

It may feel like jumping out of an airplane but do it anyway! Fly with me!

Let go of judgement. Let go of your need to figure out who is right. Let go of needing to be right. Let go of figuring out other people's motives. Let it all go!

Judgement is heavy. It's a necessary part of life because we must judge our next action. However, if you can learn to keep your judgement focused on what your next step should be and stop using it to analyze and pick the world apart trying to find what is 'right', You Will Be Free!

Judging someone can be a little thing, like getting upset at the rude person who just cut you off in traffic. Or it can be big, like your best friend betraying you by telling the world a secret they were supposed to keep. The reason these actions upset you is because you believe (or judge them) to be wrong. You believe that people should be respectful of others and careful when they drive. You believe best friends should be loyal.

So, how can you not be hurt by someone betraying you? And, even with the traffic example, how can you not be at least a little annoyed? After all, people should be careful in traffic and friends should be loyal!

Here's the Bottom Line: You can't control others. And understanding their motives won't help you. Let others do what they do without trying to judge their actions as right or wrong. Instead focus on your reaction and let what they do be on them.

I'm not saying to ignore others and force yourself to feel nothing when they 'wrong' you. I'm also, not saying to let others walk all over you. Stand up for yourself, of course.

I'm simply asking you to let go of seeing their actions in the light of 'right' and 'wrong'. Observe their actions, have compassion for your lack of understanding and have compassion for theirs, also.
Acknowledge to yourself that you Do Not Know what their journey is like and that they cannot know what your journey is like.

When we judge others, we feed our fear. When we love others, we free them from having to defend their position. We, also, free ourselves from the heavy burden of judgement!

Journal Prompt for today:
1. How can living life without judgment, free you?
2. Can you begin to practice a non-judgmental life? How would this change things for you?

DAY 20

Yesterday, I told you to let go of judgement. Today, I want to explain what this looks like in my life. I want to show you what I do to trade in my stress for adventure. Life is FUN!

I will try and illustrate my point with a story.

The other day I gave a homeless man a few dollars. He thanked me and asked me how I was. I gave the polite response of, "I'm good! How are you?". He looked at me with a hint of astonishment and said, "Well, ma'am, I'm homeless and I haven't had a shower in days." Before I could stop myself, I said something
to the effect of, 'don't let your circumstances decide your happiness. Find something beautiful, today.'

He was sweet about his response and told me he has his beautiful wife which is why he's trying so hard to gather money, so they can get a decent shower.

I left feeling like quite the insensitive soul! How could I tell someone in such a dire circumstance to love his life anyway? So, I said a prayer that my words would work as a beautiful seed planted in his heart that would grow and help him find his way to happiness. I prayed for him to follow love through his challenge and begin seeing his life as a grand adventure, instead of a never-ending trial.

Here's the deal:
I still make judgments all the time about everything. It's impossible to stay 100% judgement free. However, I'm learning to not let fear distort those judgments.

When I see something I don't like, I try and identify where my fear is messing with my view of the situation. If a child is disrespectful, I try and look beyond the disrespect and see the child's spirit as trying to navigate a very confusing world. I don't ignore the behavior. I react it to it from a place of compassion for the human condition we all live in.

When I see a 'problem' the fear strikes first. I hear the worry and the 'what now' stirring in me. Then, I redirect my thoughts. I tell myself, "Life is an adventure! Where will this take me? I choose to be excited to find out."

If I find that I'm getting stressed, it helps to envision myself as an actor in a movie. This allows me to still interact with emotion while remaining excited for how the story will play out. Doing this helps me to expect the best outcome because when I watch a movie, I fear for the characters and their circumstances but, I also trust that the writer will bring the good guy through his challenges and give him a happy ending.

Journal Prompt for today:
1. Name a problem that is really worrying you?
2. Name your favorite actor and ask yourself how they would respond to this issue?
3. Envision yourself excited as you watch your 'happy ending' playing out before you.

Don't put expectations on the how it will unfold. Just smile knowing it will all turn out Awesome in the end.

DAY 21

This week we have been looking at expectations and how they affect us.

Here's the bottom line: The only one who ever puts pressure on you is YOU.

Others may try to pressure or persuade you. But, you are the only one with the power to act. Once I figured this out my life became easy and beautiful.

You can be as light and free as a cloud in the sky!

Today, reflect on this past week and think about one thing that really spoke to you.

Journal Prompt for today:
1. What are my expectations in life?
2. Why are these my expectations and where did they come from?
3. What one expectation can I change for the better?

DAY 22

This is the final week of our 30 Days of Learning to Love YOU.

I'm more excited for this final week than any other because this week we will focus on how you can realize your infinite wealth! I'm talking about having infinite amounts of resources, love, and courage to make your life the amazing adventure it really is.

First, though, I want to make very clear that I am still practicing. There are times I fall. I let fear dictate my actions. And I forget how amazing my life is when I allow worry into my thoughts. However, when I put my focus back on my practice, I immediately feel peace. When I remind myself of all the concepts I talk about, I find my center again.

I have shared that the number one tool I use to keep my life AWESOME is mindfulness. This week I want to share how I use mindfulness to cultivate gratefulness. If you only get one thing out of this guided journaling experience, I hope it is this - Learn how to use mindfulness to stay in a constant state of gratefulness. It's the most amazing feeling of all!

When I first heard about using gratefulness to become happier, I felt guilty for not already being thankful for all the wonderful things I was taking for granted. Unfortunate people highlighted this ungrateful attitude and made me feel shame for having what they lacked.

Here's the deal: Your life is your life. It does no good to compare yourself to others. You aren't them! You are only YOU. You are only responsible for your happiness and your actions. Yes, you can love and support others but do so without comparing your situation to theirs or taking responsibility for their feelings and reactions to their life. Do no harm and love others so that their journey is better off because of you.

BUT, do not feel guilty for what their adventure holds for them. They can discover the same tools you have. They can love their life regardless of their circumstances just as you are learning to do!

For this week, as we explore how to make gratefulness the biggest part of our lives, remember to not compare yourself with anyone.

Journal Prompt for today:
List a few things you are grateful for. Then, write about why.

DAY 23

Gratefulness keeps our eyes on what is good in life. It helps us deal better with our fear, worry, and stress. When we fill ourselves up with gratefulness, we stave off the tendency to think we could be so much happier if we just had more.

It's human nature to want more. This is a basic survival instinct. It helps us to gather and store so that when times are difficult later, we are prepared. However, this instinct can lead us to be insecure, if we let it. Use Mindfulness to cultivate Gratefulness and keep this insecurity in check.

Also, as your gratefulness grows, you will feel wealthier than Bill Gates! Who I suspect, by the way, has this concept down! I believe if I did some digging, I could find evidence that much of his riches (if not all) came because of loving his life and all he had Before he became rich. But that's a discussion for another time.

For today, practice being mindfully grateful by doing the following:
1. Consider what you are using and interacting with as you go through your day. This goes for things and relationships, alike.

    o For instance, I am grateful for the laptop I use, as well as, my ability to use it.

    o When I hug my husband, I am grateful for all the good he has brought into my life.

2. Consider your five senses, being happy for the sensations they bring to your life

    o I feel the keyboard keys, as I press each one and I listen to the sound they make.

    o I completely immerse myself in the wave of sensations that come with my husband's loving embrace.

3. Consider your thoughts and emotions and feel grateful for how far you have come in your emotional growth.

   o I think of my thoughts, negative and positive, as evidence showing how far I have come in my journey because it is becoming increasingly easier to turn my negatives into positives.

   o When I feel disappointed in any relationship, I feel grateful for the opportunity to practice compassion for myself and others.

Journal Prompt for Today:

1. List a few things you are grateful for today.
2. How can you use mindfulness to enjoy these blessings even more?
3. Tonight, write about how your day went as you practiced this mindful gratitude.

DAY 24

For the remainder of this challenge we will focus on practicing mindful gratitude.

I define mindful gratitude as the practice of being present in your thoughts, actions, and sensations as you acknowledge the good and enjoy life fully.

Today, practice mindful gratitude. And, anytime you feel upset about anything, ask yourself how you can practice mindful gratitude to make the situation better.

For instance, if you find yourself running late for work, remind yourself that rushing leads to making yourself even later. Then, focus on the sights and sounds you experience on your way. Also, notice the thoughts that come to mind and acknowledge them while continuing to remind yourself that you're doing the best you can, and the world will not end even if you end up being extremely late.

Journal Prompt for Today:
1. This morning write about what you will be grateful for today.
2. Tonight, write about today's experience practicing mindful gratitude.

Love your life today, No Matter What!

DAY 25

Mindful gratitude can be used to help us work through disagreements. All we need to do is be mindful of our thoughts and the defence mechanism that tends to pop up when we feel threatened by a different point of view.

If we can learn to stop defending ourselves and simply observe, we can discover a very rewarding experience. This is because when we disagree with someone we can choose to re-examine our own perspective and view things from another person's perspective. Seeing the world through another person's eyes can be amazing!

Life is full of different perspectives. Let yourself be amazed at all the unique ways we each experience our world!

Journal Prompt for today:
1. How can you apply mindful gratitude today, particularly when dealing with difficult people or situations?
2. Notice one instance today where you disagree with someone. Apply mindful gratitude and then write about that experience tonight.

DAY 26

Paradise isn't a place, it's a state of mind. Cultivating gratefulness will bring you closer, and ultimately into that paradise state of mind!

Keep cultivating that gratitude and see if this is as true for you as it is for me! I'm betting it will revolutionize your life!

Journal Prompt for Today:
1. List five micro blessings; like Kleenex and the feel of carpet under your feet.
2. Next, list five possessions that you would really miss if they disappeared; like your car or (if you're anything like me) your coffee pot.
3. Lastly, list five people who are currently in your life or who were in your past who have positively affected your life.

For best results, use your senses as you make these lists by thinking about how these blessings affect your sense of touch, taste, smell, hearing, and/ or sight.

Go enjoy your blessings today!

DAY 27

Today, find at least a few minutes to relax and think about all you have.

Begin with the comfort in your body and the ability to breathe in and breathe out. Think about what is supporting your body as you lie, sit, or stand.

Then, look around you and take in your surroundings. What do you have that you would miss? Be happy for the convenience and care you are given by all that you have and those whom you love!

As you go through your day, make a conscious effort to enjoy all the 'little things'. Soak in the experience of birds chirping, flowers blooming, clouds passing through the sky, and every small kindness that comes your way; like a door held open or smile given.

Choose to enjoy today!

Journal Prompt for Today:
Write about how this week of practicing gratitude is going. Is gratitude helping you to love your life more?

DAY 28

Today, I want you to, again, practice soaking in your experiences.

When you hear music, focus on your eardrums and feel the music. Feel how this sense of sound affects all other sensations in your body. Feel your emotional response to the music. Fully enjoy your favorite song.

Do this when you eat or enjoy your favorite drink.

Do this when you feel fabric on your skin or hold the hand of someone special to you.

Soak life in!

Journal Prompt for Today:
1. What is your favorite scent, sound, feeling, taste, and sight?
2. Of your five senses, which is your favorite?
3. Tonight, write about your day and what you enjoyed the most.

DAY 29

Congratulations for completing 4 full weeks of Learning to Love YOU!

For Day 29 and 30 I want you to review this journaling experience.

We have spent the last 4 weeks looking at ways to love ourselves and love our lives. Look over the insights you've found while writing. And/or go back and skim through the daily posts.

Journal Prompt for Today:
1. How have you grown closer to living a life of joy and love while mindfully dealing with life's struggles?
2. What one thing have you learned about yourself this month?
3. What areas of your life are you seeing improvement in?

DAY 30

You did it! You have completed 30 Days of Learning to Love YOU!

For today, Think over the past weeks:
1. Week 1 we looked at how to turn our inner critic into our best friend
2. Week 2 we looked at how to embrace our mistakes
3. Week 3 we looked at expectations
4. Week 4 we looked at how to practice gratitude

Journal Prompt for Today:
Write about which week was your favorite and why.

60 Days of Infinite Blessings

For the next 60 days write about your blessings and what they mean to you. I have written writing prompts for each day, but feel free to either use them or come up with your own. These prompts are intended to help get you thinking about the good in your world and are not important in and of themselves. The important thing is to live a joy filled life knowing your blessings are infinite!

*Note – If you don't have some of the blessings I mention in these writing prompts please seek help and if you don't know where to look send me an email - rebeccassafehaven@gmail.com - and we'll look for help together. Everyone needs friends who love them unconditionally, safety, housing, and other basic blessings that most of us have. I dream of a world where we all have these things, and no one takes any blessing for granted.

Day 1 – Who are you grateful for?

_____

_____

_____

_____

_____

_____

_____

Day 2 – What makes you laugh?

_____

_____

_____

_____

_____

_____

Day 3 – What convenience do you enjoy the most?

_____

_____

_____

_____

_____

_____

_____

Day 4 – Which of your 5 senses do you enjoy the most?

_____

_____

_____

_____

_____

_____

_____

Day 5 – What is your favorite leisure activity?

_____

_____

_____

_____

_____

_____

_____

Day 6 – What is your favorite part of the day?

_____

_____

_____

_____

_____

_____

Day 7 – What is one blessing you can engage fully with today?

_____

_____

_____

_____

_____

_____

_____

_____

Day 8 – If your house was on fire what one possession would you

save? Why? _____

_____

_____

_____

_____

_____

_____

Day 9 – Do you have a favorite childhood memory?

_____

_____

_____

_____

_____

_____

_____

Day 10 – Enjoy a favorite food today. Consider why you like it.

_____

_____

_____

_____

_____

_____

Day 11 – Who haven't you talked to in a while? Give them a call.

_____

_____

_____

_____

_____

_____

_____

Day 12 – What was your last volunteer opportunity? What did you

gain from that experience? _____

_____

_____

_____

_____

_____

_____

Day 13 – What piece of technology do you use now that didn't exist when you were a kid? _____

_____

_____

_____

_____

_____

_____

Day 14 – Name a problem you had 5 years ago that you don't have now. _____

_____

_____

_____

_____

_____

_____

Day 15 – What is your favorite inspirational saying? Why?

_____

_____

_____

_____

_____

_____

_____

_____

Day 16 – Name 3 conveniences you love that didn't exist 100 years

ago. _____

_____

_____

_____

_____

_____

_____

Day 17 – Think of 3 small items that you would really miss if you didn't have them when you need them. _____

_____

_____

_____

_____

_____

Day 18 – Take a minute to just breathe, close your eyes, and enjoy the stillness. _____

_____

_____

_____

_____

_____

_____

Day 19 – What is your favorite comfort item?

_____

_____

_____

_____

_____

_____

_____

Day 20 – Who do you love spending time with?

_____

_____

_____

_____

_____

_____

Day 21 – What is the cutest thing you have seen lately?

_____

_____

_____

_____

_____

_____

_____

Day 22 – What is your favorite room in your house and why?

_____

_____

_____

_____

_____

_____

Day 23 - Take some time to play today. Be a kid again for a little

while. _____

_____

_____

_____

_____

_____

_____

Day 24 - Think of the miracle of electricity. What would we do

without it?_____

_____

_____

_____

_____

_____

_____

Day 25 – Google your favorite subject. How cool is Google?

_____

_____

_____

_____

_____

_____

Day 26 – Have you watched the sunset lately?

_____

_____

_____

_____

_____

_____

Day 27 – What animal is the most adorable?

_____

_____

_____

_____

_____

_____

_____

Day 28 – Who did you exchange smiles with last?

_____

_____

_____

_____

_____

_____

Day 29 – What's your favorite song? Play it and really soak it in.

_____

_____

_____

_____

_____

_____

_____

Day 30 – Who was the last person to inspire you?

_____

_____

_____

_____

_____

_____

Day 31 – What is your favorite thing in nature?

_____

_____

_____

_____

_____

_____

_____

Day 32 – If you could shop at only one store which would you

choose? _____

_____

_____

_____

_____

_____

Day 33 – What part of your health is easy to take for granted?

_____

_____

_____

_____

_____

_____

_____

Day 34 – What's the best thing about your neighbourhood?

_____

_____

_____

_____

_____

_____

Day 35 – What's the best thing about your city?

_____

_____

_____

_____

_____

_____

Day 36 – What's the best thing about your country?

_____

_____

_____

_____

_____

_____

Day 37 – Who is the most giving person you know?

_____

_____

_____

_____

_____

_____

_____

Day 38 – Who makes you feel loved no matter what?

_____

_____

_____

_____

_____

_____

Day 39 – What achievement are you most proud of?

_____

_____

_____

_____

_____

_____

Day 40 – What is your biggest blessing?

_____

_____

_____

_____

_____

_____

Day 41 – When was the last time you basked in the sun?

_____

_____

_____

_____

_____

_____

Day 42 – Take a walk. What beauty can you see?

_____

_____

_____

_____

_____

_____

Day 43 – Is your drinking water clean? Consider all that goes into bringing clear, clean water into our homes. _____

_____

_____

_____

_____

_____

_____

Day 44 – What medicine are you most thankful for?

_____

_____

_____

_____

_____

_____

_____

Day 45 – Where is your favorite place to rest?

_____

_____

_____

_____

_____

_____

_____

Day 46 – What was the last good thing that happened to you?

_____

_____

_____

_____

_____

_____

_____

Day 47 – What was your last big win?

_____

_____

_____

_____

_____

_____

_____

Day 48 – What is your favorite movie or story? Why do you like it?

_____

_____

_____

_____

_____

_____

_____

Day 49 – Who have you hugged lately?

_____

_____

_____

_____

_____

_____

Day 50 – Have you had a really good conversation lately?

_____

_____

_____

_____

_____

_____

Day 51 – Can you remember the last good joke you heard?

_____

_____

_____

__ _____

_____

_____

_____

_____

Day 52 – When was the last time you enjoyed a good piece of fruit?

_____

_____

_____

_____

_____

_____

Day 53 – When was the last time you enjoyed a cold drink (or hot)

with a good friend? _____

_____

_____

_____

_____

_____

Day 54 – What's the last piece of good news you heard?

_____

_____

_____

_____

_____

_____

Day 55 – When is the last time you didn't let fear win?

Day 56 – What is the best thing counting your blessings has done for

you? _____

Day 57 – Who can you share this magic of gratefulness with?

_____

_____

_____

_____

_____

_____

Day 58 – How has this practice of focusing on good changed your

everyday life? _____

_____

_____

_____

_____

_____

Day 59 – Has anyone noticed positive changes in you lately?

_____

_____

_____

_____

_____

_____

_____

Day 60 – Do you love yourself more today than you did yesterday? I

surely hope so! You are Amazing! I am thankful for you! _____

_____

_____

_____

_____

_____

_____

One more note page – Just because...

_____

_____

_____

_____

_____

_____

_____

_____

_____

_____

_____

_____

_____

50125593R00065